WASTELANDS

WASTELANDS

Susie Campbell

GUILL
EMOT

ISBN 978-1-913749-68-2

published by
GUILLEMOT PRESS
Cornwall
Printed and bound by Palace Printers, Lostwithiel

CONTENTS

For of Meridians, and Parallels,
Man hath weav'd out a net

—John Donne

wastelands takes place on a stretch of the Pilgrims' Way in West Surrey where the wooded hillsides of West Hanger and Weston Wood face each other across a series of ridges and valleys. West Hanger is a nature reserve whose attempt to salvage a tiny area of woodland, rare fungus, and insect-life is beset by environmental threats. Many of its great beech trees have been brought down by recent storms. It is a place of intersecting paths, some of which were walked by 'Lewis Carroll' while he was composing *The Hunting of the Snark*. Weston Wood has faced even greater threats, quarried out for its sand in the early twentieth century, and then used for landfill.

The notion of a single Pilgrims' Way, which subsumes the multiple paths and sites of an older sacred landscape, is largely due to the wishful thinking of Victorian OS surveyor Edward James but persists on modern Ordnance Survey maps.

STEIN'S SNARK

or THE ART OF NAVIGATION
(West Hanger Nature Reserve)

Navigation was always a difficult art

—LEWIS CARROLL, 'The Hunting of the Snark'

You set fire to God. A God-Tree by whose finger *here* takes shape but still you try to ignite the sacred with a spark. What is summoned always answers. It smoulders inside the rotting wood as your hands blister. Nine days in succession you return to check the blaze is out and on the tenth day the storm.

Then you fall down.

N

here is hollow as this head of rotting wood is no more than
your face on what is lost

N

lost is fallen here into death and bewildered as the empty
trunk of Knowledge is uprooted on the Path

N

a path where you fall as North is and echoes inside its
hollow navigation or any

N

and any here is always hunting for a there around this
compass

N by E

what passes as wisdom dizzies further to find the heart in a wet and torn where stood a god

N by E

to kneel before God as penitence rebukes how far the upright can fall

N by E

further than you are felled by degrees and let go

N by E

is to let go as further keeps moving and is still beyond

NNE

beyond legions along roads or crossing seas come new breeds of sheep

NNE

and the Lamb as holy familiar steps across into a new wilderness

NNE

newly willed as you face about and what is backwards if discarding the compass at this crossroads

NNE

crossing the path of a guide and fellow hunter of the difficult art

NE by N

when a hunter loses the sky path a wind from the red hills
brings familiar wet

NE by N

wandering wet is stray sheep and only a staff to protect you
or when going into the storm's circles

NE by N

as in dizzying circles drops a pair of mating buzzards you
vanish against the storm cloud's path

NE by N

and no path is right or wrong when each place is always ☜
just the place ☞

NE

this place where yesterday's root still twists against its emptiness and bends back towards

NE

or wards off fear of death with this yes and the day's flowery shrine and rattling bells empty as miracles

NE

miraculous as if you could write this in yesterday's green unnatural

NE

a natural terror if yesterday is lost in its ☜ absolute blank ☞

NE by E

blank fog if outside is a blind fetch

NE by E

and fetching in what is bare outside or shivering in doubt

NE by E

as doubting which bird trusts these feathers as if to stretch
out for flight

NE by E

then flight is to hope as inside spreads out

ENE

and light between broken branches is a door to the dead world and beetles for messengers

ENE

these messengers between Heaven and Earth as the host shelters debt in upended bottles

ENE

as shields a compass between its degrees disorientation and broken hazard tape but you anyway

ENE

and any way between subject and object searching for open loops of possibility

E by N

as close as possible to what is torn down but this is also a trackway and rough bark itches against new skin

E by N

if skin is a tender through this treacherous or feeling is bartering with danger

E by N

a danger only as this sinks its footprint in soft understorey of mast

E by N

your ☜ mast and bowsprit ☞ knitted from this tender compass

E

or compassing a hill then is a scarp where permanence crumbles even as stone is breaking at sunrise and falling

E

then the Fall brought long night to this edge a temptation but as close to Heaven and a new dawn

E

dawns beyond then and the blue scarf you knitted dissolves into someone's first glimpse of the morning

E

then you ☜ softly and suddenly vanish away ☞

E by S

a way suspended above as waiting for last night still retreats from morning

E by S

as morning summoned from above to fill empty earth with its sign of footsteps on early dew

E by S

overdue some disorder and sunrise a fresh

E by S

a rising above freshness sees as the blind horse returns to its barn

ESE

invisible bar behind whose last hope a foggy shapeshifter
pushes the glowing sun

ESE

the sum of hope hidden behind your doubt and a flounder-
ing dawn barely risen

ESE

rises behind you from fog and this trap of dead yew where
you drop your glasses and lose your way

ESE

and the way something behind you walks beside you

SE by E

beside you scuffs an invisible foot as warning crack of a dead branch and angered

SE by E

no angelic guide at your side but ketches of grinning and cast-off yew

SE by E

beside you something unfamiliar loops back to the fabric of a forest graveyard

SE by E

so many other graves and beside emptiness something hunting

SE

is hunting for a place before these traces of waiting for a grey pathless

SE

no path before those who forced their way to Jerusalem

SE

whose lament still blows through a terrible ribcage

SE

and no ribs swell heroically before a ☜ dismal and desolate valley ☞

SE by S

who watches from the valley a hundred shining wings fail
their burning burden

SE by S

a burden whose single sound longs for its echo or sacred
chord

SE by S

as a knitted cord stretched by those who hang here

SE by S

whose note repeated is proof of nought

SSE

not a foothold on this edge but a journey still drawn by
birds across the forming sky

SSE

as sky draws a prayer to prime in its first hour of daylight

SSE

and lighter than a dead leaf is none of its new growth

SSE

or groans at nothing in light fits of nonsense

S by E

none of those from a centre find what does not come back

S by E

as back to those wounded on the ground and needing prayer

S by E

are preyed upon if those are at a distance unrepeated in you

S by E

but you are those who leave ☜ not a button or feather or mark ☞

S

mark a drove road there between seasonal fairs as the swing
of wool metes heavy loops between needles

S

needing a sightline from there hunkered behind London's
defences and squeezed within compass

S

but compassed by there is now stretched by the pull in each
loop or yanking the centre

S

if no use in a centre there may be hope in a thimble

S by W

thin prospects have quarried into pit and loose stones and
no other

S by W

than other squints blocked to a narrow frontline at tank trap
or pillbox

S by W

boxing the other by compass between borders

S by W

and other is mapped over as a ☜ perfect blank ☞

SSW

earlier an imperfect map these great flints crack into stone
spread

SSW

and spreading routes network over earlier exchange

SSW

earlier and earlier for holy wild or unquarried

SSW

as quarried by later leaves no earlier

SW by S

it is earlier advance or advantage of market

SW by S

and marks it as righteous profit won by a narrow way

SW by S

the way this capital is erased from south as global North compasses it

SW by S

slides as loops along a knitting needle to its point

SW

pointing front as trampled under cloven

SW

to cleave divides and adheres for southern prospects dust blind

SW

blinkered for cycling trails and North Downs Way and Ordnance along this front

SW

or back to front is the same as both ways ☜ if it once
becomes dark ☞

SW by W

but ways to enclose a path as the way

SW by W

weights holy with protection and border

SW by W

is bordered by the authority of maps

SW by W

maps not the place but its tangled yarn

WSW

later a yearning for familiar tracks

WSW

this track left by sandals and a staff to shape a later

WSW

so later is wondering from overgrown back to wandering path

WSW

and taking this path to later is an unravelling of compass and clock

W by S

locked inside stone memory a depleted seam

W by S

seems a wayside chapel inside flint walls

W by S

as walls folded inside a series of wanderings

W by S

and inside the wandering is and and a ring

W

ringing or now echoes as an overhang allows a bowed head to pass through

W

though the hill is now a whispering mouth and its long throat of faith or testing

W

if tested now crumbles and unexpected

W

expect now in each reading and finding its way

W by N

to weigh this closeness to a dead world where the living heart pumps faster

W by N

holdfast where nesting with owls in their solitary places

W by N

these places where you find the arch of their unresolvable shadow

W by N

a shade or spirit of where the step backward

WNW

backwards from a dried-up spring will soon lose its source

WNW

as the source of soon is always ahead of no mystery explained

WNW

and plainly is not the way you have come here

WNW

for here you have ☜ wholly forgotten your name ☞

NW by W

even a name after life begins to erode

NW by W

or this road to an Afterlife just a road and this knowing a sin

NW by W

a single after cannot follow this before and before

NW by W

but after four quadrants house space or quartering time

NW

time's count of tomorrow worked on the walls of a cave

NW

as the empty cave is either a miracle or tomorrow's emptiness

NW

is empty as today's account is tomorrow

NW

and tomorrow is always beyond this hill or returning in each change

NW by N

changes that to a threshold for watching a ghost in each direction

NW by N

echoes a green chapel or cave or back to that emptiness again

NW by N

to gain a that at this reversing

NW by N

as back from that is nearly at this

NNW

where nearest is digging for some older and worms also labour

NNW

labouring back up through whose scattered bones are nearest to

NNW

or nearest which shadow splits from here and there and a smudge of moon

NNW

as the nearest shadow falls through a net

N by W

a network of marks appears beneath what is signposted

N by W

a signpost to the North Downs trodden beneath whose broken sandal or saint's fingerbone these fragments

N by W

fraying but reknitted by hand as it unravels beneath

N by W

and beneath whose breath humming as ☜ darkness comes on ☞

SNARKED

Then the bowsprit got mixed with the rudder sometimes:
A thing, as the Bellman remarked,
That frequently happens in tropical climes,
When a vessel is, so to speak, "snarked."

—Lewis Carroll, 'The Hunting of the Snark'.

there
here

DOG PILGRIM

(Map co-ordinates refer to OS National Grid reference points for Albury Landfill Site, previously Weston Wood)

Albury Landfill is situated in a large void area
Environment Agency Permit
2023

E:505623 N:148420
this site is completely lost

E:505591 N:148431
lorries loaded with waste block the sun

E:505565 N:148425
or what's lost is still alive

E:505495 N:148433
a loosening grief, violently

E:505541 N:148424
lost: spiritually ruined, fallen
or ripped away, undone
or starless, wandered from the way

... ...

E:505480 N:148434
where lying on the ground is freefall

E:505470 N:148436
systems to divide what's sacred, moves among

E:505469 N:148440
is designated empty,
wasteland, void
... ...

E:505453 N:148444
the dog doesn't care, he's dug here before

… …

E:505438 N:148451
an old mound, green barrow above a burn

E:505421 N:148457
not the dog but a bulldozer disturbs their dreams of heaven

E:505403 N:148461

no adders

left,

just the seep and hiss of gas

… …

E:505384 N:148475
dangerous love

E:505368 N:148466
invites in what was cast out

E:505351 N:148471
or wounded, wants to come home
… …

E:505326 N:148466
a fox begins the work and then the dog

E:505327 N:148465
unearths discarded carpet, decomposed matter reveals the mesh, grid
lines rot and scatter

E:505301 N:148463
what burden in the pelvis as it finally slithers free

E:505269 N:148458
the dog is already busy at other decay

E:505244 N:148459
worries at horizon's line
… …

E:505219 N:148453
obedient place
wilderness hollowed out
three churches form a protective triangle

E:505184 N:148456
wild, hurts

E:505185 N:148451
… …

E:504938 N:148174
E:504956 N:148170
E:504967 N:148167
during 1961

danger of losing the site to the quarry before excava

ever pre

E:504976 N:1481
62

E:504991 N:

E:505002 N:148 154

important area has been bulldoz

E:505011 N:148149
E:505
023 N:148145
destroyed

E:505033 N:148143
rescue excavations recorded in pencil on re-used library index cards, some missing

E:505044 N:148142
E:505052 N:148140
E:505062 N:148143
last day before bulldozers

E:505071 N:148143
E:505084 N:148149
excavating from erasure's edge

E:505052 N:148149
E:505097 N:148155
Weston Wood
mound destroyed, grid ref

erence approxim

E:505109 N:148152
E:505119 N:148149
E:505130 N:148150

mesolithic site eaten away by sand extraction

E:505141 N:148146
shall never know

E:505151

N:148145

E:505163 N:148143

E:505 E:505

171 N:148140 185

N:148140

unable to find the location

barrow

swallowed up by

E:505196 N:148135

E:505208 N:148134

E:505216 N:148132

E:505222 N:148130

the location of this site is now unknown, it is not confirmed that it ever existed

… …

E:505230 N:148132

E:505235 N:148130

obliterated

E:505241 N:148131

any trace of stone on the surface

E:505248 N:148130
stones in the south field destroyed by successive

var

ious

piec es

scatt

sc

at tt

er ed

s c a

tt er ed

… …

E:505282 N:148143
shadow of red rock
quarried away
still sings

E:505255 N:149129
decomposed voices

Chaucer, Geoffrey, *The Canterbury Tales*
(1387-1400)

Bunyan, John, *The Pilgrim's Progress*
(1678)

line

ancie

nt road

Pilgrims' Wa

this world to

come

James, Captain E. Renouard,
Royal Engineers and Ordnance Surveyor,
Notes on the Pilgrim's Way in West Surrey
(1871)

Belloc, Hilaire. *The Old Road*, illustrated
by William Hyde (1905)

soli

tary

wilder

and pits, a land

deep

shadow

of darkness to light

Cartwright Ady, Julia Mary
*The Pilgrims' Way from
Winchester to Canterbury*
(1911)

once a
wood

despera

ley
way
nets
all deep falls helving

sum

cent straightline
grim

emptiness utter s origi gho
coming of blood

De Troyes, Chrétien. Arthurian
Romances (12th Century)

Alighieri, Dante, *The Divine Comedy* (1321)

fol
loses itself

bury

cayed

hole among

dolor
fell a great
pestilence

brin brigh
water

waste forest

Tolkien, J.R.R.(trans),
Sir Gawain and the Green Knight

Mallory Thomas, *Le Morte
D'Arthur* (1485)

wretched

ston Wood

glected and marshy
close

dark
standing water

ty cisterns an

exhausted

moon

li

ght sing tumbled

Browning, Robert. 'Childe Roland to the Dark Tower Came' (1855)

narled boul
ders

green

ches

hol

low

thigh

unhealed

Eliot, T.S., *The Waste Land*
(1922)

for
est

deformed

m
ourn bleedi

wound

ende
of Engelond

to Caunterbu
... ...

E:505361 N:148186
the dog leaves a trail of dirt

E:505157 N:148450

out here for wind and sun to clean, stains crawl across the pile like shadow

E:505134 N:148455

three days of cleaning, picking off dried clods of moss and earth, mesh
comes away from pile, carpet as cleft as path

E:505114 N:148437

the dog waits for an opportunity to get even

… …

E:505086 N:148438

carpet as ceremonial hood, hod (OE), 'hodening', hooded animal
worn by guisers or for chthonic rite

E:505100 N:148420

unwound and remade is bitter in the mouth and heavy on the head

E:505085 N:148373
growling in the throat

E:505100 N:148334
strange footsteps at the door, the dog creeps back at night and whines

E:505094 N:148337
seven pieces stitched together cover the head, the rash is another warning

… …

stay away from the dead

E:505080 N:148284
needle slides easily through mesh but sticks where the carpet folds

E:505060 N:148265
worn pile doesn't forgive
… …

E:505033 N:148259
bones and a hood for travelling alone

E:505003 N:148261
tiny fragments of wing for a veil

E:504987 N:148278
needle seeks point of entry, a gate

E:504959 N:148284
all points float across a void

E:504895 N:148278
bookbinder's needle fringes wing bone, feathers, plastic twine,
phalanges nocked with coils of gold

E: 504881 N: 148268
the dog curls up to wait
… …

E:504874 N:148225
shrouded head turns, alive

E:504880 N:148238
constellations bloom on the tongue, centuries of dead skin and gassy waste

E:504882 N:148220
bone-veil swings, words fall through mesh

E:504884 N:148206
skull gapes, old gaps unbound

E:504882 N:148180
reopens wounds

E:504894 N:148177
the dog rolls in the stink of time

E:504907 N:148182
dog: to follow persistently
or broken, ugly
inferior, as in dog violet or dog rose
… …

E:505375 N:148196
words unroll a great wasteland, as unravelling, a rotting mesh of meaning frays its narrow tracks
… …

E:505377 N:148207
dog pilgrim cross-legged beneath dark moon

E:505403 N:148223
stares white-eyed, dreams

E:505464 N:148231
beneath its heavy weave, centuries

E:505551 N:148252
dog-eared, hears shadows

E:505521 N:148108
stars whisper, gape

E:505555 N:148198
between dog pilgrim's nails, fibre twists, frays

E: 505580 N: 148211
dog pilgrim yips, gives chase –

E:

50 5

60

3

N:

1

4

8

... . 2

1
2

1

E:

50

5

8

61

N:

1

8

4

2

0

1

at last, dog pilgrim comes to

an emptiness so utter not even ghosts can return

dog pilgrim doesn't care, has found holes before

tunnels   E:505654   into an older darkness   of a
waning before   the new   N:148191   having once been
walked on, wakes   this moonlit ridge   retaining these   having
once   E:505703   walked here and been   N:158216   waits for
morning's steep   to be once again   re-tongued   E:505718
or torques   the slope once mapped   having no name but
N:148257   its shadow   falls across the page   ciphered things
spread among shifting patterns so   holes as gateway   as a needle
looping   through a split   releases   or winds
or wounds   is a knot   E:505654   and what returns is
woven from an absence   is sensed   of bulldozers and broken open but
resealed   sealed surface unable to contain   N:148352   what
must re-emerge   merging syntax opens doors to   opening chambers
E:505606   and opened cells   to illegible midden   elegies of a
cindered plain   this ruined chapel's   wet sludge of violently,
bruised lilac   and cherry stains   where jostles cheap stair-carpet
N:148411   clast hunkers to hammerstone for knapping flint   debitage is
chance   words unsung   briefly a holy pool   is still a waterway
E:505262   in this hole's bright wince   where once   wells a sacred
and now   N:148131   flares, mephitic flicker   beyond the narrow
window of   what's waste become   a wider release into this
E:505286   a constant rain soaks   between sleep   and cavity's boom
N:148139   foam flakes   and what doesn't have a function
cannily re-ascends

returns

through unravelled places

undeciphered wilderness

the dog sniffs and cocks his leg

pilgrim strays

wakes, whole

WASTE POETICS

How would patterns of consumption change if we faced not litter, rubbish, trash or 'the recycling', but an accumulating pile of lively and potentially dangerous matter?

—JANE BENNETT

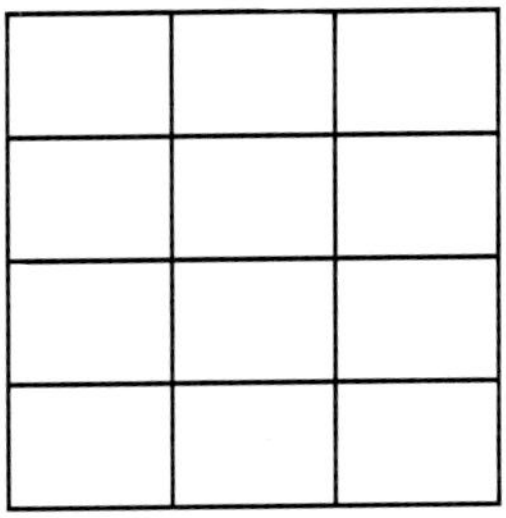

The waste mass is fully contained in a series of cells
Environment Agency Permit
2023

mashed into incoherence is an unidentifiable mass. Bubble and swell in unpredictable, erratic as the *very likeness* of what's certified contaminates or mutates. Uncased, these conjugations mate in a chemical and wildly rut

fully charged by this
dismantling, aluminium
attracts electricity in soil
where spent sap still dandles
sticky hope of life

bacchic wails welcome back
dismembered lilies and
rampant rot unwraps its
cardboard dampers for sheer
glints, sticks to cemetery
waste, seeding limp
cellophane to a new clarity

clearly is a mineral way but
hardly diaphanous. A dream
of diadems and deities
returning cold and heavy.
Garnets or pomegranate
chips are tailings, glitter fine
and orderly, such tiny
talismans of ordinary saints
lose lustre in last dustings.
Drillings from new pairs rise
in rose preens and purchases
of power

lights blue and breathless
through blown eggshells
blaze into feasting and
riotousness. Fruit rind and
potato peel banish doubts
when abundance is abandon
and frenzied on the tongue,
warm and softening or
savouring what is mixed up
and melting

changed among the undifferentiated smash of unsealed protections. Torn corners of promised each from each. New hybrids crest from unchambered seeds as this perishable performance is parsed in cardboard and polythene

wildness from a void
disperses in waves before
and after intensifies this
topple is dangerously. Such
urgent rubble inflames the
dust and broken ballast heats
and rises. Seethes in
unsteady foundations as
what's wakening draws
together, gathering in shock

and a running off to ground is distracted and lustres among dissembling metals. A malleable and ciphered modesty as base skimmings of a livelier corrosion, ductile while reanimating anode scraps, discharge blasphemously

blasted sludge greens
unnatural, leaks tears for
unripe lacks taste too early.
Or leaves in the mouth the
why and nudges of
embittered, a mildly lime
mud waste

as spectral races are flickers
in the lens of a single use and
splinters of fluff-light. Ghost
photography or flung from
life's end unsung and coming
apart of mechanical and
electronic bodies. But rises in
these phantasmal fractions
fantasies of their old purity

or ink oily and slipfast curses
de-inking sludge smears the
deceased in darkness as
dissolves these pages, pools
into a slurry of phthalo

what's thrown away lightly
wants to be worn, this
shroud to shawl and seams
what's shredded. Fibre winds
in from emptiness to
fleshing. Flexes through used
dressings or shivers, as in dry
spasms the unlit body barely
reflects its absence or
phantom gleams

HODENING

A poetic ritual for reconnecting with the waste landscape: fabric (decomposing carpet) recovered from landfill site, bones, feathers, plastic etc fashioned into a 'pilgrim cap' or traveller's hood using twine and gold jewellery wire. The hood is to be worn on site whilst keeping vigil. This is a ritual for mourning what is lost, and for honouring (or placating) the new emergent energies.

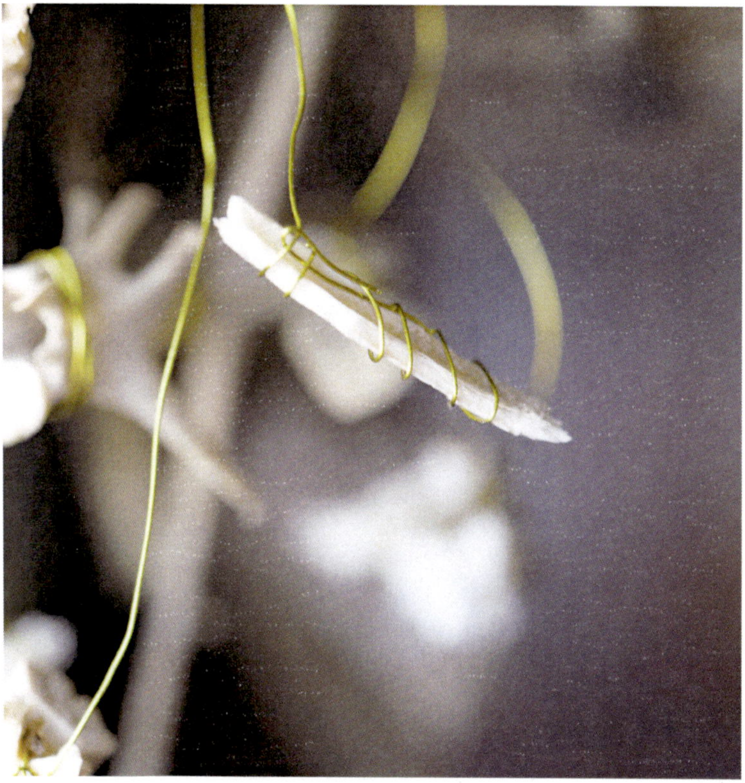

THE OLD ROAD
(West Hanger to Weston Wood)

the reconstruction of such a road is essentially the filling up of gaps

—Hilaire Belloc

it died from step
to step a wretched
way smitten, sterile
an enemy to seeds
a close, dark, and
difficult place a
rigidity of frost and
the very time in which it
died still prompts,
allures, and terrifies
whatever lingers
belongs to snow
and bare trees
possessed of a
sanctity which it has
not wholly lost the
power of the Ordnance
whereby all could
look back into the
very origins of their
blood the violence
of the compass and the
chart the first exile
is a complete
language, noise in the
dark voices
outside its community
glimpse a meaning
in things which move,

transform its
sentinels radiating
repair irregularities
and accretions are
untouched soil and
what follows from
the absence of a track
loiters where
rocks possess light

this ruined chapel of books you loved is now a sandpit, a dump

to follow a narrow way, a thin section cut through folds

is slight grammar,

is reckoned as gauze

what's loosed from the spine

in failing pages

creases the falling body

your hope's waste

held by these woods, a perilous grave

words grasp at its unseen edges

AFTERWORD

In 2022, Storm Eunice brought down one of West Hanger's oldest beech trees. A few days earlier, I had accidentally set the tree on fire. It had been a wet, foggy winter and so I had thought it would be safe to light a candle in the tree's great hollow. My ritual was dramatically interrupted by a small thread of smoke as the rotten wood caught alight. Although I quickly smothered the tiny fire, and renounced all rituals involving the use of flame, I felt profoundly implicated in the tree's subsequent destruction. Coinciding with a deep personal loss and following an episode of serious illness, its downfall resonated for me through layers of psychological, ethical, and topographical disorientation and inspired the writing of STEIN'S SNARK.

The poem is organised into 32 sections corresponding to the bearings on a navigational compass but re-oriented around an invented 'deictic' compass on which conventional bearings are challenged or replaced by 32 deictics. Deixis, from the Greek work for 'pointing', refers to those words or phrases that point to the time, space, person or situation of a piece of writing. Orienteering here becomes textual orientation. The 32 bearings are subdivided into four strands or 'pathways', each inspired by the strata of historical tracks that meet in this place. There are also ☜ 10 text fragments ☞ from 'Lewis Carroll' (Charles Lutwidge Dodgson)'s *The Hunting of the Snark* (1876).

Although West Hanger's ancient network of footways has been largely assimilated into the better-known Pilgrims' Way and the modern North Downs Way, traces of the old drovers' road still run along the edge of a prehistoric flint quarry and meet various pilgrim routes here. This drove road makes use of an even older way which connects the coast to the sacred landscapes of Stonehenge and Avebury. The nomadic drovers, who travelled this road, knitted goods to sell at fairs as they drove, using the wool of local sheep and inspiring some of my textual 'knitting', and visual experiments such as SNARKED.

Not far from West Hanger is Albury Landfill Site, previously Weston Wood. This site is in the middle of a designated Area of Outstanding Natural Beauty and is just off the Pilgrims' Way. Edward James's pamphlet *Notes on the Pilgrim's Way in West Surrey* (1871) not only enshrined his myth of a unified pilgrim road on the OS map but also inspired a colonial iconography taken up by writers and artists (such as Hilaire Belloc, William Hyde, and Julia Cartwright Ady) who romanticised this idealised Pilgrims' Way, rendering everything else, including its diverse network of prehistoric trackways and sacred sites, as 'worthless', a wasteland. This helped to prepare the way for the industrial exploitation of the Albury site, which was first quarried out for sand and then re-used for landfill and biogas capture.

Official 'rescue' archaeological excavations took place in the 1960s and identified that the site was yielding significant finds relating to Mesolithic, Neolithic, and Bronze Age settlements. Site records were kept on used library index cards and finds were stored in paper bags. Quotations used in DOG PILGRIM are taken from the correspondence and notebooks of lead archaeologist Joan Harding. In my text, they are partly fragmented and erased, reflecting the way the team worked just ahead of – or behind – the bulldozers. It is impossible to know how much more important material was destroyed.

I obtained the Ordnance Survey National Grid reference numbers for the site by walking its perimeter and entering the site itself via a public viewing platform, dropping pins using the OS phone app.

DOG PILGRIM'S opening quotation 'This site is completely lost' is from an online site of 'speculative archaeology' which specialises in locating ancient sacred sites, burial chambers, and standing stones, and identifies Weston Wood as the site of a lost cromlech and burial mound. 'Emptiness so utter' is quoted from Belloc's journal of walking the Pilgrims' Way, *The Old Road* (1905). Fragments of other literary texts are imagined as decomposing from the re-used library cards used by Harding's team. These texts all relate to various myths of a 'waste land', and its association with a wounded king/kingdom or an external or internalised quest; narratives which organise the landscape around human 'heroes', sacred objects and valueless wasteland.

My dog Charlie was an active collaborator in this project. He was himself 'thrown away' as part of an abandoned litter of newborns, and he subsequently survived by scavenging on a rubbish dump before being 'rescued'. Charlie gets excited when we visit the now-closed landfill site and it was his initial digging at the site which led to my recovery of decomposing fabric, subsequently identified as an old carpet. My commandeering of his prize and refashioning it into Dog Pilgrim's 'hod' (see HODENING) led to his constant watching and barking at the emerging, still-stinking ritual object, and his gobbling down of any small bones and feathers, also retrieved from the site, which fell on the floor whilst I was stitching them onto the hood.

I observed and notated Charlie's passage through the site, which followed very different paths and signals to mine. I have reproduced these notations in 'Dog Pilgrim'. Apparently random, they gradually emerged as purposeful although still mysterious to me.

Charlie accompanied me when I returned to the landfill site, during the darkness of a new moon, to perform a ritual meditation in situ. This involved wearing the Dog Pilgrim hood and allowing its rotting mesh, decomposing fibres, organic roots, and fringes of recovered bone and feather to reconnect me to the place - what was there, what was no longer there, and what might still be emerging.

WASTE POETICS draws much of its language from the Environment Agency's schedules of permitted landfill attached to the site permit, while the text at the beginning of THE OLD ROAD is collaged from fragments of Belloc's pilgrim journal. One of the surprises of this project was discovering the connection of both 'Lewis Carroll' and Hilaire Belloc with my own local area and the Pilgrims' Way. Local artist William Hyde, who travelled with Belloc on his English 'pilgrimage' and illustrated the book, was also, I discovered, the father of my first teacher 'Miss Hyde' who taught me to read.

Acknowledgements

Thank you to Ruth Wiggins, friend and poet, who was the first reader of this manuscript, Dr Niall Munro for his encouragement of 'Stein's Snark', Caroline Bergvall for her inspirational mentoring at an early stage of this project, and Linda Black whose *The Son of a Shoemaker* (Hearing Eye, 2012) introduced me to the use of a literary collage practice using other texts. I would also like to thank Surrey Archaeological Society and the Surrey History Centre for allowing me to access the Joan Harding Archive. Fragments from Harding's correspondence which appear in DOG PILGRIM are reproduced courtesy of Surrey Archaeological Society, with special thanks to librarian Helen Lynott. I recommend Jane Bennett's *Vibrant Matter* (2009) for further reading on 'waste' and 'the political ecology of things'. Echoes of Susan Howe's phrase 'a ciphered wilderness' (*Spontaneous Particulars*, 2014) may be heard in DOG PILGRIM and Donna Haraway's *The Companion Species Manifesto* (2003), discovered after the completion of my project, offers an alternative epigraph: 'Dogs are not just surrogates for theory [...] Partners in the crime of human evolution, they are in the garden from the get-go, wily as Coyote'. Thank you to Charlie, my partner in crime, and to his predecessor, the inimitable G.O, who died on the same day that the West Hanger beech tree was brought down by the storm.

GUILLEMOT PRESS